तेरा दीदार

शुभांजलि निषाद

Copyright © Shubhanjali Nishad
All Rights Reserved.

क्रम-सूची

क्रम-सूची

क्रम-सूची

क्रम-सूची

प्रस्तावना

तेरा दीदार 35 लेखकों का संकलन है जिसका विषय "खुला" है।
इस पुस्तक में लेखकों के अलग-अलग विचार और कल्पनाएँ हैं। जिसे वह व्यक्त नहीं कर सकता।
लेकिन इस पुस्तक के माध्यम से उन्होंने अपनी कल्पनाओं को शब्दों से सजाकर कविता के रूप में प्रस्तुत किया है।
तेरा दीदार शब्द का अर्थ है किसी को निहारना, जिसे हम बहुत प्यार करते हैं, बस उसे हर पल अपनी आंखों के सामने देखना चाहते हैं।
वो शख्स जब भी हमसे दूर जाता है तो हम अपनी कल्पनाओं में उसका चेहरा ढूंढते रहते हैं।

प्रकाशन के बारे में

वइर्स ऑफ सोल एक राइटिंग कम्युनिटी है, जहां हमारे पास नए नवोदित लेखकों का एक समूह है, जो भावनाओं को शब्दों में ढालने की अपनी प्रतिभा के साथ हैं।

उत्साही लेखकों को प्रोत्साहित करने और उनकी सराहना करने के लिए 15 मई 2021 को डॉ. निकिता दुदागी और लकी पांडे द्वारा गठित समुदाय के सर्वश्रेष्ठ लेखक को पहचानने के लिए साप्ताहिक विशेष कार्यक्रम और कार्यक्रम आयोजित किए जा रहे हैं। वइर्स ऑफ सोल, महत्वाकांक्षी लेखकों का एक समूह जो पाठक के मन को प्रेरित करने के लिए अपने दिल की भावनाओं को स्याही करता है।

वइर्स ऑफ सोल पब्लिकेशन केवल एक प्रकाशन नहीं है, यह लेखकों का एक प्रकार का परिवार है जिसमें सह-लेखक, लेखक, लेखक, संकलक,

सह-संकलक, ग्राफिक टीम, परियोजना प्रमुख, सीईओ, सह-संस्थापक और संस्थापक शामिल हैं। यहां हर कोई अपने विचार देने के लिए स्वतंत्र है और हम उनके कार्यों की पहल करते हैं....

• x •

1. Shubhanjali Nishad

Compiler

ये नाम शुभांजली निषाद है इनका जन्म 21 दिसंबर को उत्तर प्रदेश के जिले कानपुर में हुआ था । वा इन्होंने अपनी शिक्षा सीजेएसएम यूनिवर्सिटी से पूर्ण की है यह पिछले 5 सालों से लेखक के तौर पर काव्य शायरी लिखती आई हैं ।इनको लिखने का काफी शौक भी है वा इनकी रुचि हिंदी काव्य लेखन में भी काफी समय से रही है। अथवा यह इस पुस्तक "तेरा दीदार♥?" की

संकलन कर्ता भी है । वह 500+ से अधिक संकलनों में सह-लेखक के तौर पर भाग ले चुकी हैं और उन्होंने दो संकलन भी किये हैं इनकी पहली संकलन पुस्तक का नाम "किसान" और दूसरे संकलन का नाम "फीलिंग्स ऑफ हार्ट" था । इन्हें लिखने के साथ ही पुस्तके पढ़ने वा नई जगहों पर घूमना भी अधिक पसंद करती हैं । वह सभी प्रकार की कविताएं लिखने में रुचि रखती है । और उन्हें कल्पनाओं में भ्रमण करना पसंद है उन्हीं कल्पना पर मद्द के माध्यम से ये अपने विचारों को कोरे पन्नों में अपनी रचनाओं को खूबसूरती से लिखने कि हुनर रखतीं हैं और इन्होंने अपनी कविता लेखन की माध्यम से कयी रोज़ाना काव्य प्रतियोगिता में भाग लिया है एवं ये कयी प्रतियोगिता में विजय भी हुई है ।

इनसे संपर्क करने के लिये Gmail I'd

nishadrock96@gmail.com

Insta I'd- kanha_ki_laado.

तेरा दीदार ❤?

मरहमी सी तेरी आंखें देखने को जी चाहता है।

जब भी मैं देखता हूं तुझे नकाब ऐ पोश में,

कमबख्त मेरा दिल जल सा जाता है कैसे बताऊं,

मै तुम्हे ये दिल कितना चाहता है मैं भी बंया करना

चाहता हूं अपना इज़हार ऐ इश्क लफ्जों में पर,

तुम्हें देखते ही मेरा दिल थम सा जाता है ।

बस तब मन में एक ही ख्याल आता है ,

काश ये मेरा एक ख्वाब सच सा हो जाता ।

तुमको गले से लगाना संभव हो पाता काश!

मै भी तुमसे अपने दिल की बात कह पाता ।

क्या है मेरे दिल में तुम्हारे दोस्ती के सिवा

कुछ और भी जज्बात है मेरे दिल में जो

मै अपनी दिल की सारी कश्मकश को,

तुम्हारे साथ सुकून के दो पल बिता हर,

एक बात को बड़े सलीके से साझा कर पाता ।।

2. Mona Mahajan

Mona Mahajan is a 19 year old young adult with stars behind each eyelid and dreams to sore high in sky. This drew people close to her endless heart. When she felt her wings were clipped she realised that it's always in your darkness that stars start to appear. Thus she began her journey to pour her soul in her poems .

Childhood Memories

I see my childhood in stars

And find all those leftover scars.

Behaving like my teachers always ready to mend.

Shooting starsmemorize my fav racing car

Crossing the pleasant voice played by guitar.

Playing stars attract me towards them,

Realising that childhood was a gem.

Shining stars make me rise,

So that I can grow thrice.

3. Shibani Mishra

She is Shibani Mishra hailing from Bhubaneswar, Odisha. She's 15 year's old zoophilist and her hobbies are writing and photography. She was featured in Times Of India for a write up and mostly posts on Instagram. Contact with her through Gmail I'd shibanimishra2006@gmail.com and insta I'd @sassyshibani

FANTASIES

Waiting for my muse to come,

I start to wander around.

Took some new turns,

And somehow I ended up

In the crazy place they call

Lost and found.

There I discovered things so rare

That once were surely handled

With delicacy and underlying care.

Some dried petals,

Some unfinished battles.

Some handmade cards,

Some misplaced regards.

Some lost charms.

Some cold words that still felt warm.

Some shattered dreams;

Brand new.

Some broken hearts,

Maybe more than a few.

Some childish games,

Some inextinguishable flames.

Some tattered feathers,

Some dreaded weathers.

Some preserved drops of rain.

Some attempts in vain,

Which would have led to undying pain

And driven everyone insane.

In the end it didn't matter

How I stumbled upon them,

Cuz every single one

Was a precious gem.

4. Subhanjali Dutta

Subhanjali Dutta, a writer and poetess by passion, was born in West Bengal, India and brought up in Guwahati, Assam. She loves weaving poetry out of human emotions and subtle feelings. Inspired by nature, she leaves bits of serene beauty of nature's treasure in her works. Currently a NEET aspirant, Subhanjali aspires to spread love and positivity through her poetry.

Drifting apart

Though things between us have changed,

I'm still awestruck by the startling similarity in our bond,

With a touch of subtle drifting apart,

Till date, no matter how much we try,

To friendzone each other,

We end up falling for each other's soul,

It's a phase of latent pain,

Faking smiles, breaking ourselves,

Both ending up empty handed,

We long for each other's arms,

To find solace,

Somewhere, something keeps stopping us,

From letting our vulnerable self,

Get the better of us,

Unknown reasons guide us,

To pretend to be strong in front of each other,

It's funny how both of us can see,

Right through the façade of lies,

Know the story of each other's bare heart,

The story both of us are,

So afraid to believe.

5. Vidisha Mohanty

She is Vidisha Mohanty from Bhubaneswar, Odisha. Her hobbies are sketching, travelling, dancing. She is a new writer but didn't participated in any social media contest yet. But she is now writing a story and soon going to be complete. Contact her through Gmail I'd vidi24mohanty@gmail.com and insta I'd @itzz_me_vidi.

Heart break

The way that makes me deep down sad,

Which makes me feel a little bad,

Deep down inside me is something makes me
uncomfortable,

Which I show that it's the reason I smile,

Having a great memory with you was like a dream of mine,

And after that now those memories are only hurting,

Making those cuddles and spending time together all went
like a dream,

And now those dreams made me heart broken?.

6. Akshita Aggarwal

अक्षिता अग्रवाल एक कवयित्री, लेखिका और कई संकलनों की सह-लेखिका हैं। वह दिल्ली से हैं और अपने सबसे अच्छे दोस्त और कोई नहीं बल्कि अपनी कलम के साथ अपना समय बिताना पसंद करती हैं। जब वह अपनी कलम के साथ नहीं होती है तो वह अपना समय प्रेम कहानियां, उपन्यास पढ़ने और संगीत सुनने में बिताती है।

फुर्सत के पल

सुनो ना,

बहुत सारी बातें करनी है तुमसे।

कभी तो तुम भी,

फुर्सत के कुछ पल चुरा लो ना।

माना कि आजकल,

पहिए लगे हैं सभी के पाँव में।

पर,

बिताने को तारों की छाँव में,

कुछ वक्त तो चुरा लो ना।

बहुत सर्दी लगती है मुझको।

कभी तो तुम मेरे लिए,

अपने हाथों से अलाव जला दो ना।

फिर भी सर्दी लगे जो मुझको,

तो एक ही कंबल मेरे साथ ओढ़,

मुझे अपनी बाँहों में भर लो ना।

अगर लगूँ तुम्हें कभी,

थोड़ी परेशान सी मैं।

तो मेरे माथे को चूम लो ना।

मैंने क्या-क्या किया पूरा दिन?

कभी तो साथ बैठ पूछ लो ना।

तुमने कैसे बिताया अपना दिन?

मुझे अपनी बाहों में भरकर बता दो ना।

माना कि करती हूँ कभी-कभी,

ज़िद बहुत सारी।

पर तुम्हें तो हूँ ना मैं,

बहुत ज़्यादा प्यारी।

तो कभी-कभी,

थोड़ी ज्यादा-सी ख्वाहिशें पूरी कर दो ना।

नहीं मांगूंगी मैं कभी,

चांद-तारे या सोना-चाँदी।

बस कभी तारों की छाँव में,

एक शाम मेरे संग बैठ जाओ ना।

बहुत सारी बातें करनी है तुमसे।

फुर्सत के कुछ पल चुरा लो ना।

✍?अक्षिता अग्रवाल✍?

Insta Id - akshita22072000

7. Shahista Agwan

एक साधारण उभयचर लड़की जिसका नाम शाहिस्ता अगवान है। वह मुंबई शहर की रहने वाली हैं। वह अपने विचारों को कागज पर उकेरती थी और उन्हें अपने पास रखती थी। लेकिन अब उसने कुछ पाठकों के साथ साझा करने का फैसला किया, इसके लिए वह यहां हमारे साथ इस उम्मीद में हैं कि उनके पाठक उनके पहेली तरह के शब्दों को समझेंगे क्योंकि उन्होंने सह-लेखक और राष्ट्रीय पत्रिका के रूप में कई पुस्तकों में काम किया है। जल्द ही अपनी सोलो बुक लॉन्च करने वाली हैं।

एक तरफा मोहब्बत

वो भी मुझसे बहुत प्यार करती हैं,

लेकिन यह बात वो मुझसे कहने से डरती हैं।

वो शरमाते हुए थोड़ा गुस्सा भी करती हैं और,

वो कहती हैं हमारे रिश्ते का नाम सिर्फ दोस्ती हैं।

लेकिन, यह हमारे बीच दोस्ती तो नहीं हैं क्योंकि,

उसकी आँखों में भी मोहब्बत साफ झलकती हैं।

जितनी बातें वो पूरे दिन में मुझसे करती हैं ना,

उतनी तो वो अपने घर वालो से भी नहीं करती हैं।

जितनी खुश वो मेरे साथ पानी पूरी खाते हुए होती हैं

उतनी तो वो पिज़्ज़ा-बर्गर खाते हुए भी नहीं होती हैं।

और अब मैं कौन से लफ़्ज़ों में बयान करू,

उसकी दोस्ती नाम में छुपी हुई मोहब्बत का।

वो पगली अपने किताब के आखिरी पन्नो पर भी,

सबसे छुपा कर सिर्फ मेरा ही नाम लिखा करती हैं।

जितनी मोहब्बत से वो मेरा ख्याल रखती हैं ना,

इतना तो वो कभी खुद का खयाल भी नहीं रखती हैं।

वो अपनी मोहब्बत छुपाने की कोशिश तो करती हैं,

लेकिन उसकी शर्माती हुई आँखे सब बयान कर देती हैं।

वो भी मुझसे बहुत प्यार करती हैं,

लेकिन यह बात वो मुझसे कहने से डरती हैं।

8. Noor Tabassum

The name of the author is Noor Tabassum. Writing is her passion. She is an author in Scribe Mag magazine and a blogger in Times of India. She is also a regular poet in Muse India- my space. She has participated in more than 350 anthologies. She has also written solo books called 'Sensibles', 'Twisted Firsts' and 'Adorable prod.' She is a nature lover and loves to lead a simple life. She expresses all her feelings in her writing as she thinks it is the most powerful medium to communicate. Her thoughts and writings are appreciated through a lot of competitions.

Option or priority

Life is an enthralling challenge divided between priority and option,

Coming into this world was the topmost priority given,

But how we dominate our lives is an option.

Adorning your lips and tongue with kind words is a choice,

But then you become the precedence to the ones whose hearts you touch,

The way you earn your living is a preference,

But the possibility to make a lawful morsel should be a priority,

Thousands are surviving on the planet as a criterion,

But only a few make it their priority to dictate the hearts.

A fragile transparent string lies between option and priority,

When you love someone, see that you are their priority, not an option,

When you become a priority, you become leaders of the heart,

Or you end up becoming a slave to their wishes.

Our heart is a devoted slave but a tyrant commander,

Always opt to maintain your desires under control and enjoy
the devotion,

Death is an unpleasant certainty which we must confront,

But before that, make a meaningful life your option.

9. Ashrita Dash

She is Ashrita.....a girl being witty with curly hair and writes poem when sleepy...or studying or being yelled by mom.... Everytime wandering in the world of imagination....she loves to to dance, sing or studying.....everyone loves her and she too loves everyone.....

A story

Hey …I am Kylie. I am a doctor. I lost my one leg when I was young. So today let me tell you one of my saddest yet happiest story. I was studying in class-7 and I had already lost my right leg. Before I lost I danced well , in sports everyone cheered…. Kylie! Kylie! But now I have just to see my friends running….Than…one day happy news came to me. My father said let's take her to City hospital and let she have a metal leg.After 1-2 days I had my own but metal leg. Than after 1 month of rest I got up and was able to walk by my own leg..not to take anyone's help. I was happy. After I went back to my house…I went with my mother to my friend's house. Then my friend Lily called all my friends.. Avalon, Lily,Forysthia,Mary I had all…but than after sometime when my mother went to Lily's mother for chatting…They closed the door and told jokes about me that were unresistable…but I kept quiet and made a face that no-one has seen ……but they kept joking until my mom came and they started to be very well behaved for me…Then I went home…and cried so much that no-one can understand. Than after I went to my village and I thought that people in village would behave well..but when I went some far from them after talking they would tell "See…that helpless girl… can't do anything just sitting all day …I heard from her mother ..she doesn't studies…I don't know but it's very difficult for her to manage it…" And then when my mother and father were busy for something and I was sitting and reading a book some boys came and pushed me from my wheel-chair..i got injuries... until I call someone they vanished...from that day I got so much angry that I forgot that I had lost one leg. After reaching home I studied hardly and I passed my exams with flying colours....and there was not a competition in which I was not a winner....than after from people I heard Again my name coming out of their mouth.......Than 1 day principal of the school called me and asked question"Child how you managed all these??? Than I said "Sir only love yourself"....

10. Manish Gupta "प@rth"

इनका नाम मनीष गुप्ता है यह एक कवि हैं और कविता लिखने में ज्यादा दिलचस्पी रखतें हैं । कवि yourquote पर भी अपना कविता को लिखते रहते है । कविता के माध्यम से वे प्रेम ,वात्सल्य प्रेम , जीवन की डगर पर ज्यादा संजीदगी से पेश करते है । 22 वर्षीय कवि जीवन की कठिनाईयों के साथ साथ वास्तविकता पर ज्यादा जोर देते है । फिलहाल कवि B.Ed के छात्र अध्यापक है ।

प्यारी प्राणप्रिये

मुझे आज भी सुहाती हो तुम

मुझे आज भी नज़र आती हो तुम

मेरे मन में उत्साह भर देती हो तुम

मुझे आज भी दिल से लगा लेती हो तुम

सपने तो बहुत देखे ,

अरमानों मे दिख जाती हो तुम

प्यार किया मैंने तुमसे

बाद मे मान भी जाती हो तुम

सच बताऊँ तुमसे ज्यादा प्यार

किसी से नही किया मैंनें

फिर भी मुझे प्राणप्रिये

मना कर देती हो तुम ।

11. Ranbir Bhakat

Author by heart and passion.
Writing since He was 16.
Ranbir Bhakat is pursuing an integrated undergraduate course in Commerce from Calcutta University, Kolkata. His writeups touches reality and reaches everyone's heart. He wants to grasp and grow in his writing journey. His poems can please your broken heart and also please your emotions. Wrote about 400+ Anthologies & 2 Solo Book in preparation.

A REASON YOU'RE ALIVE

This is for all those people

Who hide in the dark,

For those who feel hopeless,

For those with a broken heart.

This is for every child and teen

Who is trying to flee from their fears,

For those who cry themselves to sleep,

For those who drown in their tears.

This is for people who hide their scars

Upon their wrists and their thighs.

I want to remind each of you

There is a reason you're alive.

You are here for a purpose;

You are needed in this place.

You are special, you are beautiful.

It doesn't matter what size, gender, or race.

12. Har Deepansh Bahadur Sinha

हर दीपांश बहादुर सिन्हा लखनऊ, उत्तर प्रदेश से संबंध रखते है। इन्होंने नैशनल पोस्ट ग्रेजुएट कॉलेज से भूगोल में स्नाकोत्तर की शिक्षा ग्रहण की है।

गाने सुनना, पकवान बनाना , गाड़ी चलाना इनकी रुचियाँ है। लिखना , तस्वीरे लेना , सौरमंडल को समझना और घूमने के प्रति इनका गहरा लगाव है।

मर्द की दास्तान

वह भी है एक साधारण इंसान

है उसका भी ज़मीर और ईमान,

उसे भी चाहिए हम सबका सहारा

जिम्मेदारियाँ निभा रहा बेचारा ।

उसकी भी हैं कुछ इच्छाएं

समाज ले रहा उसकी परीक्षाएं,

मेहनत करके परिवार को खिलाता

ज़माना उसपर क्यों दबाव डालता ।

सब मर्द एक जैसे नहीं होते

कभी कभी वह भी रो लेते,

छुपा लेता है अक्सर वह अपने दर्द

कौन कहता सारे एक जैसे होते मर्द ।

उसके जीवन में भी ढेरों कठिनाईयाँ

हस्ते खेलते भूल जाता परेशानियाँ,

कौन कहता है उसकी ज़िंदगी है आसान

ज़रा एक बार लगाकर देखो उसपर इल्ज़ाम ।

वास्तविकता में यही है मर्द की परिभाषा

यदि जो लगी उसके हाथों निराशा,

तुरंत हाथ छोड़ देता है समस्त संसार

क्यों होता उसके साथ यह व्यवहार ।

13. Bhawana Agnihotri

इनका नाम भावना अग्निहोत्री है।
ये रायपुर शहर की रहने वाली हैं।
इन्हें कविता लिखने का शौक है।
इन्होंने रांझणा" कहानी लिखी है।

तुम्हारे लिए

मैं मोहब्बत में बड़े बड़े वादे तो नहीं कर सकती, मगर हां मैं हर शाम तुम्हारे लिए अदरक वाली चाय बना सकती हूँ, हां मैं कभी कभी बदतमीज होती हूँ, मगर तुम्हारे लिए मैं तहजीब सिख सकती हूँ, हां मुझे इस मॉडल ज़माने में बाकी लड़कियों की तरह बाबू सोना कह कर अपना प्यार जाहीर करना नहीं आता, मगर में इस मॉडर्न जमाने में पुराने ख्यालात की लड़की तुम पर सैकड़ों कविताएं लिख कर आओ अपना प्यार जता सकती हूँ, मैं वक़्त की पाबंद हूँ मगर इस 4g से भी स्पीड चलने वाले डिजिटल जमाने में, मैं सुबह की शुरूआत से लेकर रात के आखिरी पहर तक तुम्हारा इंतेज़ार कर सकती हूँ मैं।

अब तुम सोचोगे ऐसा क्यों ?

तो सुनो.....

शख़्त से एक दिल में एहसासों की हरकत होने लगी है,

बावरी सी रहने वाली एक लड़की अब इश्क़ में सँवरने लगी है।।

14. Karan katiyar

करन कटियार उत्तरप्रदेश (कानपुर) में बिल्हौर के निवासी हैं, अभी कक्षा १२ में पढ़ रहे हैं। इन्हे कविता लिखने का शौक पिछले 4 साल से है। इन्होने काफी कविताएं लिखी भी है और वो इनकी स्वरचित कविताएं किताबो में प्रकाशित भी हुई है।

तेरा दीदार

करता हूं दीदार तेरा

चाहता हू देखना हर वक्त तुझे

नजरो से दूर हो न मेरे

देखू तुझे हर शाम हर सवेरे

कितनी अहमियत है तेरी जिंदगी में मेरी

ये तू खुद जानती होगी

नहीं जानती तो पता कर लो

जिस दिन नही दिखती है

कितनी फिक्र होती होगी तेरी

याद आती है तेरी मुझे यहा

और हिचकी आती होगी तुझे वहा

इतना विश्वास है मुझे

करता हू दीदार तेरा

कि जब नही दिखती है तू मुझे

फिक्र होती है मुझे

तू दूर न हो नजरो से मेरे

सामने रह मेरे,सामने रह मेरे

प्यार चाहिये मुझे जीने के लिये

जरूरत है तेरी प्यार पाने के लिए

15. साबिया रब्बानी

इनका नाम साबिया रब्बानी है ये वाराणसी शहर उत्तर प्रदेश की रहने वाली है, इन्होने संजय मिमोरियल वूमेंस कॉलेज से बी ए सी बॉएओटेक्नोलाजी से ग्रेजुएसन पास किया है। इन्होने बहुत से एंथोलाजी में हिस्सा लिया है कम्पाइलर और सहलेखिका के रुप में। इन्होने खुद का दो किताब भी लिखा है जिसका नाम दोस्ती में प्यार है, और दूसरी हमारी जिंदगी है ।

इनको आप YouTube channel Sabiya Rubbani के नाम से देख सकते हैं और Instagram per aliyah-khan-1 के नाम से

खोज सकते है।

हुआ जब से दीदार उसका

वह हुस्नो सबा रंग लाने लगा,

मंन में हलचल मचाने लगा,

हुआ जब से दीदार उसका,

ये दिल भी उसका होने लगा।

कैसे रुकू इस तूफान को भला,

जो मुझसे ही मुझे उड़ाने लगा,

ना जाने क्याँ बात वह तुझमे देखा,

जो एक पल में ही तुझे अपनाने लगा,

इस दिल को भी बहुत रोका,

मगर वह भी तेरे लिए धड़कने लगा,

जो कल तलक अनजान सा लगता,

अब ना जाने क्यूँ अपना सा लगने लगा,

जब भी होता दीदार उसका,

नम आँखे भी मुस्कुराने सा लगता

और जब से मेरे साथ वह रहता

तब से हर गम दूर सा लगा ।

16. Sukanya Biswal

She is sukanya Biswal .She is Coordinator in EPSON.
GRADUATE FROM Adv Post Graduation Diploma in
Computer Application.
She is passionate of Photography.

Role of Life

It is not so easy to play the role of life,

A person has to be scattered in order to reconcile the relationship.

It's just a matter of feelings, otherwise,

Love does not happen even after seven rounds.

Heart meets heart, people punish

People drown the feelings of love,

How can people see two human beings meeting,

When people blow away even two birds sitting together.

17. Amarjeet Singh

अमरजीत सिंह का जन्म और पालन-पोषण ग्राम-लखमारी, जिला-कुरुक्षेत्र (महाभारत की भूमि) में हुआ है। वह अंबाला कैंट में कॉलेज के छात्र हैं। वह अपने शब्दों में सच्चाई लाता है। उसे नाटक खेलना, माइक खोलना, बागवानी करना और कविता लिखना पसंद है। वह एक सह-लेखक के रूप में 93+ एंथोलॉजी का हिस्सा रहे हैं और कई दैनिक कविता चुनौतियों में जीत हासिल की है। अब वह दो अलग-अलग समुदायों में काम कर रहे हैं। आप इंस्टा पेज पर जा सकते हैं: poe_try9826

एम्बुलेंस

बोलते मुझे एम्बुलेंस सारे,

हर दुख में लोग मुझे पुकारे।

कभी कोई मुझ में से डेड बॉडी उतारे,

तो कभी देते मरते को सहारे।

102 नंबर पे कॉल करते लोग,

मेरे आते खत्म हो जाते रोग।

देख लाल बत्ती रास्ता देता सारा संसार,

किसी दिन उनका भी हो सकता है इस में परिवार।

सुनते जब सायरन की आवाज,

करते लोग दुआ सब आज।

खुशियों को मैं वापिस घर लाती,

लोगो में जीने की उमंग जगाती।

चौबीस घंटे रहती तैयार,

लगाती दिन में चक्कर सौ बार ।

18. Juliet Hudait

Juliet Hudait is a 15 year old who's passionate about Photography, Music and Writing. She is from West Bengal and currently lives in Bangalore. She is a Bibliophile and an Astrophile. She has co-authored 560 books and she's the compiler of 22 books. Connect with her on Instagram @juliethudait

SHY FACES

Remember the first time we met,

On a Saturday evening?

The calm weather,

The warmth of the candles,

The enlessness of the sky,

The smell of the roses

And our shy faces?

None of us could look straight into each other's eyes.

We kept looking at each other for a second and then
turning away.

Those shy smiles we gave each other,

Those silly things we did due to nervousness,

All of those will forever hold a special place in my heart.

19. Muralidhar Bansal

ये नेपाल के मुरलीधर बंसल हैं। उन्हें लिखना बहुत पसंद है और वे छात्र जीवन से ही लिखते आ रहे हैं। वह बी कॉम है। वह वर्तमान में व्यापार में लगा हुआ है।

उन्होंने अपने करियर में आत्म-प्रेरणा के साथ लिखना शुरू किया। वह समय के अनुकूल होने तक लिखित रूप में अपना हाथ जारी रखना चाहता है।

आंखें

कितनी प्यारी यह आंखें होती है

आसपास दोनो साथ रहती है ।

हर भावनाओं में यह कुछ कहती है

कुछ अनकही अनजानी बातें अपने तक रखती है ।।

बहुत कुछ यह सहती है

जैसे सायद कुछ कहना चाहती है ।

दोनों एकसाथ यह सोती है

एक को हो कोई परेशानी तो दोनों ही रोती है ।।

इतनी सुन्दर की जैसे कोई मोती है

इनमें जैसे अदभुत एक ज्योती है ।

सारा गम अपने अश्क से धोती है

हर खुशी मे उल्लास बोती है ।।

साथ कैसे रहना यह तालमेल दर्शाती है

जो भी मिले यह दोनों वह साथ पाती है ।

मुझको तो लगती यह जैसे दिया-बाती है

ओर कुछ न अब तारीफ मुझसे जताई जाती है ।।

20. Rahul B R

He is Rahul.B.R

He was born in 19/09/1999 Ramanagara district, Karnataka.

But he is perceiving his higher studies in Bangalore. He has completed bachelor degree in science. He like to know more about literature and want to study more and more about it...

He started writing poems from past four years and he writes all kinds of poems... on life, about nature's beauty, love and much more. He is coauthored in many books, Compiler of the book called "The Song Of Nature", "Nemophilist", "The Song Of Paradise",

"Wings To Your Thoughts", "The Unchosen Bond" and "You Are Mine" and also his poems has been published in his college magazine too.

YOUR SIGHT

I am always in your sight,

Even for the true fight.

I never let you down,

Till the end of mine.

You are always mine,

I want to see you fine.

Until the last the end,

I will be with you as a friend.

Your happiness is mine too

Except that I have no clue ,

What to do

And what not to do....

21. Arpita Saxena

Arpita Saxenais a teacher.she has completed her schooling from KVS. She is post graduate in MSc geography along with diploma in disaster management.she had a decade experience in banking and insurance sector. She loves to explore history and admire nature.she loves content related to history geography and culture.

Miserable Masterpiece

I can not be bound to some traits,

I have a personality that with itself debates.

I can not be caged,

I have a soul that knows no barricades.

Certainly, its hard to explain,

However, my fixed trait is, trying to explain when its totally vain.

Somedays I love all, other days I like none,

I wish to blame it on hormones,

But you cant put it all on them, comeon.

Somedays I wish meeting everyone alive,

Other days, I wish no one could see my alive.

Somedays, I say it all out loud,

Otherdays, in my own head I get knocked out.

Its not hormones, it never was,

It was always where your life at that point on you took a
toss

None can always be bubbly,

If you are, then you are pretentious like me.

Its not possible to always love,

When deep inside your own identity for you is blurring off,

Its easy to say " be positive",

But reality is that positive is positive because there is
negative.

You cant always neglect it.

We can never be ideal,

Because humans are only meant to be real.

I am no one to preach

But yea, that's me,

I am not perfect, just a miserable masterpiece.

22. Kajari guha

Kajari Guha,M.A B.Ed with a glorious teaching background, is a published author.She has written several books for the students of Communicative English and a memoir named Bridging the gap—Shatarupa,published by Partridge publishers.This book is still available with Amazon.in Writing is her passion and writing poems has become an obsession with her.She has earned numerous accolades for this on social media.She hopes that the readers would enjoy her creations.

She is a translator and has a command over three languages i.e. English,Hindi and Bengali.

She had been a casual artist in Patna AIR(Sitar Instrumental).A composer of several songs that are viral on YouTube "Writing is her goal.Music is her soul."

Eyes speak a lot!

Eyes speak a lot..!

They create many slots!

Love is the foremost tale!

The eyes charm and also tell!

The stories capsuled in the

Tricky glare!

The onlooker is trapped

Easily in the snare!

The blinking eye can

Be really ominous!

Some feel scared

Some stay joyous!

Eyes may be green

With envy!

Anger makes eyes

Red hot gravy!

Like the blooming lotus

The eyes open up slowly!

Like the setting sun

They close suddenly!

May God grace all eyes

With soothing light!

To get rid of evils that

Spread darkness in life!

©Kajari Guha

23. Keerthi Priya M

She's Keerthi. She is a proud individual from Karnataka. She has been a compiler and co-author of more than 100 anthologies. Apart she's interested in photography, gardening and art.

Coffee

A day without coffee would be like,

A garden without roses for a few,

Their day begins with a cup of coffee,

Coffee smells aromatic,

And tastes sweet with sugar.

The estates of a coffee,

Are indeed an example of scenic beauty,

With the springing, fresh, green leaves,

And the red blooming beads,

Looking beautiful,

Yet bitter to taste.

Cherishing the monsoon,

In the coffee estate,

Indeed gives great pleasure.

©Keerthi Sonu

24. Bishakha Kumari Saxena

बिशाखा कुमारी सक्सेना जी ग्रेटर नोएडा की निवासी हैं और पटना से इन्होनें अपनी सारी शिक्षा पूरी की है। ये समाजशास्त्र में स्नातकोत्तर की उपाधि प्राप्त की हुई है । इनकी रूचि कुकिंग, कविता लेखन, पेंटिंग, फोटोग्राफी में है । घर की जिम्मेदारी के कारण नौकरी को छोड़ दिया था । तो पूरी तरह से अपनी रूचि की तरफ ध्यान देना शुरू किया। इन्होनें कुकिंग के प्रतियोगिता में अनेक मैडल, ट्रॉफी, प्रमाण पत्र हासील कर रखा है। इनकी कुकिंग

में किताब भी छ्प चुकी है । लेखनी में भी मैगज़ीन और 100+ किताबों में इनकी रचनाये छ्प चुकी है। ये अच्छे विचारो को अपने लेखनी के माध्यम से लोगों तक पंहुचाना चाहती है ।

चांद रात और तुम

चाँद रात है और तेरा इंतज़ार है

मिल जाओ ईद के बहाने,

अँखियो से करना तेरा दीदार है।

चाँद रात है और तेरा इंतज़ार है

आ जाओ उसी चौबारे पर,

जहाँ पर हमारे मिलन का आसार है।

चाँद रात है और तेरा इंतज़ार है

कितने जन्मों से नशा है तेरा,

अब तो ये नादान दिल बहुत बेकरार है।

©Bishakha Kumari Saxena

Insta:@bishakhakumarisaxena

25. Jasmine Panda

Miss Jasmine Panda is presently pursuing Ph.D. in Synthetic Organic Chemistry as DST INSPIRE Fellow in Ravenshaw University, Odisha, India. She is a Gold Medalist and University Topper in both her B.Sc. and M.Sc. from Berhampur University and has been awarded from Odisha Chemical Society for her excellent performance. She was also the M.Sc. Entrance Topper in BU. She has successfully completed an internship CSIR-SRTP in IICT

Hyderabad. She holds the post of Senate Member of Berhampur University for the session 2019-20 in Academic Pursuits. She is a Governor Awardee for Youth Red Cross. She has received All-Rounder Award in her 12th standard for excellence in extracurricular activities along with studies. She is a Topper throughout her career. She has been Literary and Cultural Champion in her school, college and university days. She has also cracked a campus in Vedanta.

She has hosted in numerous events including International events and has been appreciated as an anchor. Besides PGDCA, she has also completed Masters in Fine Arts (MFA) from Aurobindo Kala Bhawan under Bangeeya Sangeet Parishad, Apart from being a versatile orator and debator, she has been a part of 1000+ anthologies till date and loves to pen down her feelings! Some of her co-authored books have achieved the title of "OMG Book Of Records", "Indian Book of Records" and "Forever Star Book Of World Records". She looks forward for compilation and publication of anthologies. She has compiled an anthology "VASUDHAIVA KUTUMBAKAM" under SOI publication which is also the best seller#9. Another compilation with an unique concept of "SMILE PLEASE" is well-appreciated. "HOPE OF A MASKLESS FUTURE" under NLHF Publication is also an awesome Compilation of her. "LESSONS FROM EXPERIENCES" is another compilation which has gained popularity among the readers. She has been a winner in numerous National and International events and conferred with the priviledge of many titles. Many of the reputed organizations such as Akhil Bharatiya Vidyarthi Parishad (ABVP), Chhatra Sandesh (Odisha), Rashtriya Kala Manch (India), many National and International Rotaract Organisations, The Inked Perceptions, Hum Foundation, etc. have acknowledged Her talent. She has been honoured with 1100+ certificates by God's grace. She is an amiable person interested in both Science and Literature, having a wide variety of interests like painting, sketching, crafting, interior designing, acting, anchoring, debating, rangoli making, taking part in extempore, clocution and many more...Publishing her own book someday is something which she deeply aspires.

The Pillar Of The Strength

With good character and striking personality,

Youth, an amazing inspiration for everyone!

With team work and leadership qualities,

Can be an extraordinary example for someone!

Continuously striving for advancement,

Be it technologically or scientifically!

To stand, to fight, to attack, always ready,

Possess a strong spirit of nationality!

With real power and undefined strength,

Youth, the backbone of the nation!

Following all rituals, ceremonies and morals,

Be it our past tradition or the new western!

Disciplined and dedicated in their work,

Best at handling situations everytime!

Focusing on strengths, working on weaknesses,

Out of hardships and struggle, they shine!!!

In any situation, be it worse or worst,

Not a lover of war, but peace, peace & peace!

Always come forward with positive spirit,

To save their country, their power never seize!

Utilising their capabilities to utmost extent,

Having a realistic ambition and fulfilling it!

Their life is for them to self-introspect,

Along with living for others, the divine reality!

"Pen is mighter than the sword", rightly said,

Hence, understanding the value of education!

Must keep the name and fame of the country,

To gift everyone a lovely place to sustain!

Youth, the pillar and symbol of strength,

Youth, the ever-achieving and ever-changing!

Honesty and humanity they should possess,

Their life will always be ever-rewarding!

26. Jyoti Verma

इस लेखिका का नाम ज्योति वर्मा है ।ये बलिया उत्तर प्रदेश की रहने वाली है

इनकी उम्र महज सत्रह साल है ।

इन्हें लिखने के साथ साथ डांस में भी बहुत रुचि है और इन्होंने बहुत प्रतियोगिता में भी भाग लिया है जिसमें ये अवल भी रहीं है ।

ये अभी सिर्फ बारहवीं पास है ।इन्हें खेल खुद में भी बहुत रूचि देखी गई है । इनके परिवार में सिर्फ इनके माता पिता और इनका एक छोटा भाई है ।

इनके पिता का नाम संजय कुमार वर्मा है जो कि एक बिजनेस मेन है और इनकी माता हाउसवाइफ है ।।

इनका छोटा भाई अभी क्लास नवी में है ।

आगे ज्योति बताती है कि इन्हें ,,,प्रकृति ,, देखने में बहुत रुचि रखती है ।

यू तो है दूरियां

यू तो है दूरियां हम दोनों के बीच बस जगह की ,

पर दिलो में दूरियां कहा , दूर रह कर भी करीब है ।

ना जाने हमारे दिलो में कितने लोग का बसेरा है ,

पर जिसका नाम आकाश है, उसके जैसे कहा कोई है।

तड़पते है हम मिलने को एक दूसरे से ,

पर इन तड़प में प्यार और गहरा होता जा रहा है ।

तेरा यू हमें बच्चा बोलना , किसी बात पर गुस्सा हो जाने पर ,

तेरा लाखो तरीके से मनाना ,

मानो दुनिया की सबसे बड़ी खुशी है तु ।

तलब तो है बहुत तेरे जीस्मो की खुसबू में समा जाने को,

पर सच्चा प्यार हर किसी को मिले ये जरूरी नही।

तड़पते है हम आकाश को अपने आंखो से करीब देखने को,

पर इन खोज भरी आखिया मे,उनकी प्यार की gahraiyaa और बड़ती चली जा रही हैं।

तलब है इन हाथो को , तेरा हाथ पकड़ने को

पर एक बार ये दोनों हाथ मिल गए तो क्या अलग करना आसान होगा
।

रूह करती रहती है इंतजार तेरा ,

इन कानो में झुमके पहनाने को,

तेरा पसंद के कपड़े पहनने को,

रह गई है बस आस तेरी इस बिड पड़ी दुनिया में।

27. Mahvish Mishra

इनका नाम महविश मिश्रा। कलम नाम
"intheworld_of_goodvibes" के साथ लिख रही हैं। ये सुंदर और
सबसे पुरानी जगहों में से एक "वाराणसी" से संबंध रखती है।
इन्होंने बहुत पहले अपने विचार और विचार लिखना शुरू कर दिया
था और अब ये एक लेखक हैं । इनका पसंदीदा शौख लेखन एक
जुनून बन गया। ये उद्‌धरण, ब्लॉग और लेख लिखत हैं इन्हें
लगता है कि कई और चीजें हैं!, लेखन मेरा पहला और हमेशा के
लिए प्यार है। इन्हे लगता है कि हर किसी को एक खिंचाव की
जरूरत है, इसलिए मैं अपने फ़ीड में आप सभी का स्वागत करना
चाहती हूं अच्छी तरंगे!!

लम्बी जुदाई

महीने भर के लिए बिछड़े थे,

पर साल गुजरने को आई।

कहते थे एक पल भी जी नहीं सकते

अब तो बस साथ है तन्हाई

कभी रोज़ मिलने की ज़िद करते थे

अब मीलो की दूरी भी नहीं खटकती

कहना आसान था, कि कभी ना बिछड़ेगे जिंदगी भर के लिए,

वो किए वादे तो अब याद भी नहीं आते

ख्यालों में आपके हमारा हर साल बराबर था

कभी हर गम हर खुशी बांटा करते थे

अब तो बात करने के लिए भी तरसते हैं

साल भर में शायद ही कोई पल बिता था

जब तुम्हें देखने के लिए आंखे ना तरसी हो

अब तो कोई नजारा भी नहीं भाता

पता नहीं अब कब तुमसे मुलाकात हो

न जाने हम से क्या हो गई खता

जो किस्मत भी हमसे रुठ सी गई

जिसको सुबह शाम दिल में बसाते थे

उनसे ही मिली हमें सबसे लंबी जुदाई।।

28. भावना मोहन विधानी

अमरावती निवासी सौभाग्यवती भावना मोहन कुमार विधानी को बचपन से ही लेखन का बहुत शौक रहा है। उन्होंने अपने लेखन का सफर कक्षा सातवीं से बाल कविताओं के रूप में शुरू किया। उन्होंने अब तक काफी सारे लेख शायरी कहानियां कविताएं लिखी है, जो काफी सारी पत्र-पत्रिकाओं में प्रकाशित हो चुकी है। उन्होंने कई बार ऑनलाइन कवि सम्मेलनों में भाग लिया है। लेखन के साथ-साथ भावना जी को बागवानी कुकिंग और गायन का शौक है। भावना जी ने शादी से पहले सहायक शिक्षिका के रूप में भी कार्य किया है। भावना जी को सोशल वर्क में भी बहुत रूची है। वो अमरावती की कई सामाजिक संगठनों से जुड़ी हुई हैं। उन्होंने

अपने घर में एक छोटा सा किचन गार्डन बना कर रखा है उनका मानना है कि सबके घरों में पेड़ पौधे होने चाहिए।

"एक कप चाय"

चलो मिलकर एक साथ फिर वो पुराने पल जीते हैं,

एक गर्म चाय का प्याला फिर एक साथ पीते हैं।

गर्म चाय की तरह पुराने पलों की गर्माहट को ताजा करें,

आओ फिर एक साथ मिलकर हम अपने राज साझा करें।

जिंदगी की भाग दौड़ में हम जीना ही भूल गए हैं,

अपनों को पीछे छोड़ अनजानी राहों में निकल गए हैं।

चलो फिर एक बार पुरानी राहों पर लौट चलते हैं,

बचपन के पुराने दोस्तों से फिर गले मिलते हैं।

चाय के प्याले के साथ कितने किस्से जुड़े हैं हमारी यादों के,

वो दोस्तों की महफिल और दिन हंसी वादों के।

अब सब अपनी अपनी दुनिया में मशगुल हो गए हैं,

वो प्यार से बंधे दोस्ती के रिश्ते को तोड़ से गए हैं।

चलो भूल जाते हैं सारे शिकवे गिले हम अपने,

एक गर्म चाय पहले के साथ फिर साकार करते हैं अपने सपने।

मिलकर बैठते हैं आज दोस्त सब एक साथ,

पुरानी यादों के साथ साथ लेते हैं गर्म चाय का स्वाद।

29. Kamini Pradhan

कामिनी प्रधान, पिता- श्री मंगल प्रसाद प्रधान , माता -श्रीमती तपोवंती प्रधान , जो ग्राम पंचायत -आमगांव, शाखा -तमनार, जिला -रायगढ़ छत्तीसगढ़ से रहने वाली हैं, जो अभी एम. एस .सी रसायन शास्त्र में अध्ययनरत है, जो पढ़ने लिखने के साथ ही संगीत में रुचि रखती है ।

तेरा दीदार

जब से मेरे नैना तेरे नैनो से लागे तो लगे कुछ नया ,

तब से मेरे जीवन का हर पल हुआ सुनहरा ,

लग गई लगन अब रातों को चैन कहा ,

सोते जागते इस आखों में तेरा ही दीदार जहा ,

मत कर मुझे तेरे रंग में शामिल में डूब गई तो,

मेरे सामने तुम न होते हुए भी परछाई शामिल रहेगी ,

तुमसे हमेशा मिलने लगी हु सुनहरी रातों को ,

जो ख्वाब में मुझे हमेशा सताया करते है ,

मेरे ख्वाबों में आकर अपना ही रंग शामिल कर जाते है ,

मेरी सुबह की एक सुकून वाली नींद तेरे ही अमानत होती है ,

जब से तुमसे दीदार हुआ है , मेरे अहसास में तुम्हारा नाम रहा है ,

तुम मुझे ऐसे सताते हो और मेरी मुस्कुराहट बन जाते हो ,

इन आखों ने तुम्हारी आखों में एक राज देखा है ,

कसम से मैने इन आखों में तुम्हे पल पल आज देखा है ।

30. Meera Gopalakrishnan

Meera Gopalakrishnan published a novel Seven Vows(under the pen name Shruthi) and two short stories Second Chance and The Forgiveness I seek as Meera. She has also co authored 53(28 as Shruthi,25 as Meera) anthologies so far. She is an active member of 6 writing communities and an English Judge in three writing communities. She is currently into Podcasting also.Before becoming a writer, she was working in IT industry. She loves Indian mythology, culture and Indian history and interested in weaving stories around that. She has an active profile in Wattpad shruthiravi13 and her insta id is mira_g_pai

My Beloved

The crowd is so huge for the festival,

But my eyes are searching for only one face.

Sound of the bhajans fill the air,

My ears are only yearning to hear one voice.

Lights are sparkling in the festive ground,

And I am looking out for the sparkle of her smile.

Stage was set for the dancers to show their skill,

My wait for her footsteps seemed endless.

As if my prayers were heard,the soft voice fell in my ears.

The sound of my name in her lips was the sweetest gift I
could ever get.

The crowd disappeared and the stage stood still.

The silence of the night engulfed me as I looked into her
face in the moonlight.

The scars given by acid were still fresh on her face,but my
eyes only saw that pure heart.

She had wanted love, but all she got was lust.

Today for that broken woman I want to gift the world and let her know the meaning of love.

31. Mr.heet

इनका नाम हीत है और ये जमोधपुर जिले से संबंध रखते हैं
लेखन इनका पसंदीदा शौक है ।

सोच समझकर ठुकराना हमें

हम वो है जो बार-बार मिला नहीं करते

कोई सुनने वाला नहीं हो तो गिला नहीं करते

इश्क मिजाज़ी लोग हैं

मोहब्बत के बाद नफरत का

सिलसिला नहीं करते टूटे हुए फूल खिला नहीं करते

फटे हुए रिश्ते को सिला नहीं करते

जो नहीं हूं हमारी आशिकी से खुश

हम उन्हें हमारा हक दिया नहीं करते

सोच समझकर ठुकराना हमें

छोड़े हुए जीते रहते हैं

अपने भले की दुआ नहीं करते

जी लेते हैं हक से

मोहब्बत में बर्बादी का सिला नहीं करते

सोच समझकर ठुकराना हमें

एक बार खो देने के बाद हम दोबारा मिला नहीं करते

32. Dr. Aditi Dev

"इनका नाम डॉक्टर अदिति देव है । ये फ़रीदाबाद जिले की निवासी है । ये एक होमीओपैथिक डॉक्टर हैं तथा इन्होंने मास्टर इन हास्पिटल अड्मिनिस्ट्रेशन सें पोस्ट ग्रैजूएशन किया है। इन्हें लिखने के साथ साथ चित्रकारी में भी रुचि हैं।यें प्रकृति से लगाव भी रखती है।इन्हें प्राकृतिक जगह पर घुमना बहोत पसंद हैं।

"पैरों के निशां"

रेत सी हो गयी है ज़िंदगी मेरी,

पैरों के निशां भी मिट से गए है ।

तुम्हारी आहट भी सताती है मुझे,

आँखो के अश्क़ भी सूख से गए है ।

वो प्यार भरी बातें करना तुम्हारा,

अब तो बस अल्फ़ाज़ ख़ाली रह गए है ।

मिलना हमारा अक्सर यूँ छुप छुप कर,

अब नैना मेरे , तुम्हारे दीदार को तरस गए है ।

खाईं थी क़समें हाथ थामें रखने की ,

मगर अब वो ख़्वाब अधूरे रह गए है ।

सोचा था निभाएँगे साथ ज़िंदगी भर हम दोनों,

मगर अब वो एहसास जुदा हो गए है ।

33. Tapaswini Mohanty

Tapaswini Mohanty a student of class VI is a accomplished author and co-author who has worked in many anthologies. She is currently learning "Korean language" . She is also a artist.

My world of dreams

Everyone has a dream to achieve in his/her life. Some people dream of becoming famous, popular and rich whereas some want to make others happy by helping them. My dream is to become a IAS officer. I have seen many IAS officers who risk their life for their country. I feel very proud of them and always think that one day I'll also become like them.

Dreams are just like flowers, we can't imagine our life without them and such as we take care of our flowers like that we should care for our dreams. It is the driving force that energizes us to do each and everything to achieve it. This proves that:

"Believe in your dreams. They were given to you for a reason."

34. Deval Chhatbar

Deval Chhatbar is a teacher and also a content writer. She is from Gujarat, India. She was a student of IT but her keen interest in teaching led her to different path and she became a teacher. Besides teaching what attracts her is poetry. So she started writing poems and started exploring the field.

She writes stories and poems in Gujarati, English and Hindi. As the IT industry had left its impact on her, she is technology lover. She believes in doing maximum task digitally including her job.

Anyone wants to catch her poems, needs to visit insta page: a_corner_of_her_heart.

FRIENDSHIP

YOUR FRIENDSHIP IS IN MY HEART,

YOUR CARE IS IN MY MIND,

I HAVE TRUE LOVE IN MY EYES,

BUT THE FACT IS I CAN'T BE YOUR WIFE

BECAUSE

SOMEONE IS ALREADY IN YOUR LIFE!

IT IS BETTER TO BE NOT SO NICE,

LET'S END THE RELATION WITH A GREAT FIGHT!

LET YOURSELF TO HATE ME,

UP TO THE LAST BREATH OF YOUR LIFE....

35. Sana Noel Murray

Sana Noel Murray is a 17 yr old student belonging
from Nagpur Maharashtra,
She's a writer, compiler and a motivational speaker

Travel

I don't travel much, but when I do I enjoy it to the fullest looking out from the window of the train is one of my most favorite things in the entire journey, that's when I also realize that as we move to different cities we see different people from different cultures and hence I admire the beauty of India, even though we are from the same country we have different cultures at different cities and states. Being from different cultures we remain with the same bond and brotherhood and proudly adress ourselves as "Indians". Playing family games while in the train is something which gives me great nostalgia , finally when we reach our destination exploring the different places and having food which is a bit apart from the day to day food that we eat is something that helps me to get out of my comfort zone and be more diverse, and of course how can you just come back without shopping ! Buying gifts for family and friends is something that gives me happiness and joy that I can't explain!

Travel is something I wish to do a lot more…

_Sana Murray

36. Ritu Gupta

Ritu@Ritz, A Simple Person with a thousand dreams in her heart. A Survivor since the start, she faces the storms that are sent to tear her down. A teacher and a Counselor by profession with a motto to serve the World, she has bagged many prizes and recognitions in the field of Education, Art, Photography, Music and Social Work. She has a passion for travelling and dancing. Loves cooking and is a Crazy Brat but doing harm to none. Believes In Spreading Smiles And

Positivity Around!
Her Mantra is,
"You May See Me Struggle,
But You Will Never See Me QUIT!"

"IS YOUR EGO STOPPING YOU FROM MAKING THAT APOLOGY?"

No one can make the right choice or decision every time in their life cz NO ONE IS PERFECT. Sometimes even with our best intention, we make wrong decisions that can hurt our loved ones.

When a person is hurt, they need to be healed. Apology helps to heal because it makes that person feel that you understand their pain. It raises your respect in their heart. But when a person feels that you are unapologetic, it breaks them even further. Apology can be hard especially for those who are egoistic as they see apology as an insult to their personality. But apologising doesn't make you any less than anyone. In fact, you get a peaceful feeling in your heart no matter what the outcome. So once you realise your mistake, make an honest effort to apologise as that's the right thing to do.

Never step away from apology if you are wrong. However hard it may seem, apologising takes only a short time but if you lose the person and the relationship, you may regret for your entire life.

37. Manisha Haldar

Manisha Haldar is the Writer , Poetess and Pranic Healer from Madhya Pradesh. She is the would be Doctor . She writes to spread awareness , positivity , humanity , equality , peace , truth happiness and love.

Equally valuable

My success is equally valuable.

As much as a boy's success matters.

My dreams are equally valuable.

As much as a boy's dream matters.

My existence is equally valuable.

As much as a boy's existence matters.

My freedom is equally valuable.

As much as a boy's freedom matters.

My identity is equally valuable.

As much as a boy's identity matters.

My decisions are equally valuable.

As much as a boy's decision matters.

My goals are equally valuable.

As much as a boy's goals matters.

38. Mahima Mishra

महिमा मिश्रा 16वीं साल की लड़की हैं। 11 साल की उम्र से ही उन्होंने लिखना शुरू कर दिया था। उसकी प्रेरणा का स्रोत उसका परिवार है, विशेष रूप से उसकी माँ और वह उद्धरण, कविताएँ और लेख लिखना पसंद करती है। वह सोचती है कि लेखन आपके सबसे अच्छे या बुरे विचारों को सामने लाता है।

मेरा पहला और आखिरी प्यार

दिल की धड़कन मेरी सदा है तू

मेरी पहली और आखरी वफा है तू

चाहा है तुझे चाहत से भी बढ़कर

मेरी चाहत और चाहत की वजह है तू

तुम नहीं जानते कि कितने प्यारे हो

तुम जानते हमारे और जान से प्यारे हो

चाहे कितनी भी दूरियां हो हमारे दरमियां

तुम कल भी हमारे थे और आज भी हमारे हो

सितम सारे हमारे साथ लिया करो

नाराजगी से अच्छा है डांट लिया करो

फरमाइश की है दिल ने भी

लिख दूं मैं एक नई कहानी

साथ मेरे तू हो और मेरे अरमां भी

जी लो हर एक लम्हा तेरे संग जानी

तकदीर से चुराकर कस्टम को सजाया है

हमने एक ही जहां बनाया है वह भी तुझ पर लुटाया है

तेरे साथ रहने की तलब है अब तो खुदा को भी

यह बताया है

मरना नहीं जीना है तेरे साथ

हमने तो पूरी कायनात को यह दिखाया है

घायल करके मुझे उसने पूछा

करोगे क्या फिर मोहब्बत मुझसे

लहू लहू था दिल मेरा मगर

होठों ने कहा बेपनाह बेपनाह ।

39. Binod Dawadi

He is Binod Dawadi from Purano Naikap 13, Kathmandu, Nepal. He has completed his Master's Degree from Tribhuvan University in Major English. He likes to read and write literary forms. He has created many poems and stories. His hobbies are reading, writing, singing, watching movies, traveling, gardening, etc.

He likes pets. He is a creative man he does not spends his time by doing nothing. He is always helping for the poor people. He can't see the troubles and obstacles of the people. He believes that from the writing and from the art it is possible to change the knowledge and perspectives of the people towards any things. He loves his country Nepal very much. He has known many cultures of his country as well as foreign countries. He is always thinking wisely towards any things. He solves his problems by using his mind. He dreams to be a great man in his life.

Your Lover

I am your lover,

I love you more than me,

I can't give you luxury,

I can't give you stars,

Of the sky or,

I can't prevent you from sick,

As well as from dying,

But I have good heart which loves you,

More than anyone in this world,

Believe me in my words how can I prove to you,

I want to care you,

I want to spend my time,

With you,

I am your lover,

Besides my love what,

Do you need in your life,

I am your lover,

Who do mad love which,

Is true and spiritual love,

To you,

I am your lover.

40. Apeksha khedkar

Apeksha Khedkar , She is a Writer And Poetess. She Is 14 years old girl ,from Pune. She Born in Ahmednagar In 2007 . She is in 9th Now .She is a Co-author in many Anthology's And Compiler of Love you Mom and compiling more . She is working in many communities and Publications as judge , technical head ,graphic designer , manager and project head . She started writing from past 2 years .She writes Poems ,Shayari, Stories, microtales And Articles in 3 language English ,Marathi and Hindi on love ,life

,nature beauty ,success and many more! It feels her connected to herself as she explore herself every moment. Inking her emotions and feelings is the best company of her life .

She is featured on many newspaper , website , instagram pages, youtube channel and also she is on Spotify. She has won many poetry & writing contests. Writing is her passion .And She is Also A Great Dancer. She loves to make sketches.

Her aim is to achieve success in short time!

To contact her - Instagram I'd - @words.of.apekshaa

You Know

You know

Everything in my life would be dull without you,

Because I have alots of love for you and it's really true.

You know

I want to describe my love for you,

But I can't so I started writing poems about you.

You know

Your lovely Smile fills my day with joy,

And I can't stop thinking of you my boy.

You know

I Can't live without you Because I love you,

And now I have to thank God for giving you.

You Know

This silly heart has fallen for you ever since it first saw you.,

There is no boy out there like you.

You know

I will never change my feelings that I've for you,

And I don't want to imagine a life without you.

You Know

You are never far from my thoughts and from my heart,

Our love for each other is so strong that no amount of
miles can ever affect it.

You Know

I'm just craving for you

And I know no one can love me like you.

You Know

I just want to spend my all time with you,

Just stay here don't go anywhere.

41. Rangeesh Chandrasekar

Rangeesh Chandrasekar is a MBA Finance and Marketing graduate staying at Chennai. He is passionate about writing and a great lover of books and articles who has Co authored in 800+ anthologies and compiled 8+ anthologies.

My Kanha

I love to be alone , than in a bad company

But I am not alone , I have Krishna in my company

I and My Kanha (Lord Krishna) are always together

Whether it's a sunny day or rainy weather

Whenever I am in a trouble

With his help, I overcome every struggle

Whenever I felt left out

He helped me every time to stand out

He is the reason for every fortune

He stops every misfortune

He is my Kanha, my brother

A cute brother from another mother

He is the one who wipes my tears

He is the one who whisper in ears

He is the one who is the reason for my life

He is the one around whom revolves my life

I and My Kanha will never be apart

We are like 2 souls in a heart

Still you think that I am alone

I won't prefer your company but loves to be alone